MW00790058

A Voice

TURNING PAIN INTO POWER

A Voice

TURNING PAIN INTO POWER

HAVVA RAMADAN

Black&White

Black&White

First published in the UK in 2024 by
Black & White Publishing Ltd
Nautical House, 104 Commercial Street, Edinburgh, EH6 6NF

A division of Bonnier Books UK
4th Floor, Victoria House, Bloomsbury Square, London, WC1B 4DA
Owned by Bonnier Books
Sveavägen 56, Stockholm, Sweden

A CIP catalogue record for this book is available from the British Library.

ISBN: 9781 78530 707 2

1 3 5 7 9 10 8 6 4 2

Typeset by Black & White
Printed and bound in Great Britain by Clays Ltd, Elcograf S.p.A.

www.blackandwhitepublishing.com

Dedicated to

Ilker Ramadan

Sad are the hearts that love you
Silent are the tears that fall
Living our lives without you
Is the hardest thing of all

Author's Note

If you are here reading this then you have supported
my mind or my heart in one way or another and I just
want to take a moment to say thank you. No matter
how many times I thought I'm not gonna make it
through this one, I did, and I need you to know you
can too. I hope my words bring solace to your heart,
the way you have brought solace to mine.

I appreciate you.

Contents

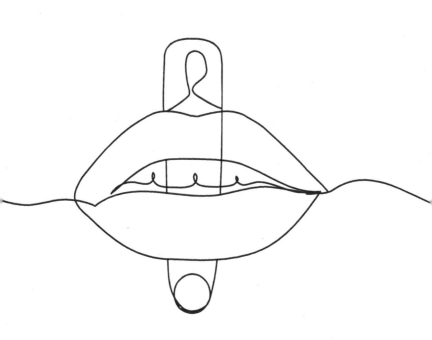

Ask God Why

I think I will ask God

"Why"

For the rest of my life

And never will I come to understand it

Even if God himself stood in front of me

And told me the reason

I don't think I would accept it.

Some loves are too hard to bear

And with great love comes great pain

And with great loss,

Comes the greatest pain of all

If love could have saved you

You would have lived forever . . .

2 Faced

Do you know how many times I've taken an 'L' and just nodded ok?

Or how many times I've replaced a whole text with 2 words, instead of an essay

Do you know how many times 1 tear has rolled down my face when I realise that

REAL EYES REALISE THE REAL LIES
And I REALISE

I wasn't worth the truth and I ate your lies because my heart was hungry

And how many times my pain is shattered pieces of *"I thought they loved me"*

How many times I took betrayal on the chin and I took greed, wrath and envy from the rehearsal of their 7 deadly sins

I stayed humble when I watched the people I love stab me in the back

And I took that knife and cut them off with it and forced myself to not look back

I don't wear my pain on my face but it's written in my eyes

And if you speak the language, you'll identify with mine.

Chosen

And I wondered what it was like . . . To be *CHOSEN*.

I was never *CHOSEN* . . .

I was a maybe, a probably, sometimes even a definitely but never the one.

Never the *CHOSEN* one.

As I grew up I realised the mistake I had made was to wait to be *CHOSEN*.

By Him or by Her or by Them.

I wasn't even choosing me so why would anyone else choose me?

So now I simply don't wait.

I don't wait for a man to notice me and I don't wait for a girl to choose me.

...*I CHOOSE MYSELF*

How Come

―――――――――

How come?

The best of us leave this earth too soon while the bad
seem to live forever
The ones we love the most are gone and all you can
do is try to remember

How come?

It's the happiest people with the biggest smiles that
tend to carry the most pain
They cry inside while dedicating their lives to making
sure WE don't feel the same

How come?

The prettiest people are the most insecure, we tend to
think of them as God's favourites
They're deceptive of self and neglected because well . . .
Why does a beautiful person need help? And that's
the danger

How come?

It's the kind hearted that tend to carry the most pain

it's insane, to be kind is a gift we all deserve

Yet, when you're kind you're more of a target, don't you think that's absurd?

How come?

The good die young, that's how the saying goes and

it's proved to be true time again so it shows

that the devil is here and this can't be the end

for the best ones are taken to heaven so young . . .

. . . How Come?

Excerpt – Story of Dad

I always struggled with the idea that living is forever. It seemed too long to me, so overwhelming. You mean I have to be here until the end? Trapped in this mind of mine. I may as well be in prison. Because there was no way out for me. A million eyes crossed mine and not one of them noticed, I mean really noticed. Maybe I was just too good at hiding it. Or . . . maybe it wasn't real. It was all just in my head. "Yes I KNOW!" I would reply. But how do you show someone that something is real when you have no proof? You're highly functioning. Life and soul of the party. That can't be true.

Until one night my heart was ripped out of my chest . . . and everything that once made me sad disappeared. How trivial, you silly stupid girl. Life taught me what real sadness was. I spent so many years wanting to die not realising how much I had to live for. Now I have to struggle to stay alive, with so much pain to die for.

It didn't beat again.

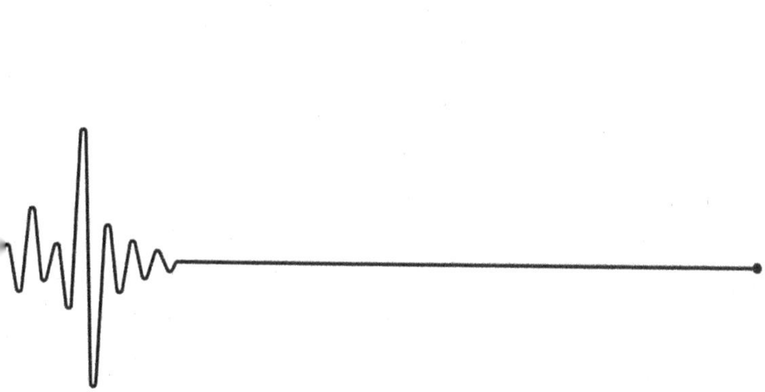

Fathers

When referring to the Fathers
We speak of the unspoken Hero
For there are no limitations on the lengths
A Father would go
To protect, to provide and to the children
He is the biggest man in the world
They look at him in awe and they feel
Safe when he is home

The unspoken is the Father
For he wears that cape every day
But along with it comes a mask and no matter
How tough things get they never say
We take them for granted most days
Because they never let us down and we get
So used to what they do for us we don't think to
Offer anything in return

A Father's love is silent but it's the most
Powerful of all, they're our greatest teachers and their
Hug could break you, but it also makes you stand tall
Sometimes they go unnoticed and the way they
Struggle gets so suppressed
But no matter which one of us you ask we say

"

My Dad is
the best...

"

Betrayal

Betrayal is the hardest of the emotions to deal with

Because it never comes from your enemies more like the people you live with

You can be in love one day and be heartbroken the next

Someone can whisper forever to you in one moment and destroy your nest in the next breath

And when you look at them you think, how could you do this to me?

While the constant narrative of *why wasn't I enough?* plays on repeat

You look in your kids' eyes and you feel guilt for letting them down

Even though it wasn't you that's left their little faces upside down

But you know what my favourite saying is:

"God will put you right back together in front of the people that broke you"

And no it won't be easy but I promise you one day they'll think about the things they did to you
And when your light is shining so bright that the Wanderer can't help but want to return to the Pack

Take a look at the little faces you turned around and promise yourself you won't look back.

More

And should they stop loving you one day
I hope you know that it was nothing to do with your
capacity to be loved but their own capacity to live up to
the expectations they had built within the love they had
displayed unto you.

I hope you know that it does not make you unlovable, it
just means that this love is no more

but that you will be more without it.

Extraordinary

You don't need to be *extraordinary*
to not be *ordinary*
You just need to be you
and keep it in your mind's eye
that there's nothing you can't do

There is no one with your genetic makeup and especially
not your DNA
you are created one time only
and you will never be created again

To be *ordinary* would mean to be
the same as everyone else
but it's impossible to be the same

The only similarity you might have is the
sharing of your name
But a name is not *who* you are
it's just what you're called it's a title
but it doesn't categorise you or place you in a box
and really it's so vital

That you understand this statement:

You are a limited edition a one-time only, never to be recreated again

You are extraordinary just by existing – because no matter how many lifetimes pass,

You
 Will
  Never
   Exist
   Again

999

She said **999** what's your emergency?

I said my heart hurts

She said *that's not a crime Miss*

I said but it should be, how is it not criminal that someone can tear apart a beating heart and live freely?

She said *I don't know but it's not something I can help you with*

Then who can? Who can help because the pain in my body feels like it could break me yet you're telling me it's not a crime committed because there is no external infliction

You want cuts and bruises on my body in order to take my name but cuts and bruises to my mind and my heart don't seem to be enough?

It feels like an emergency. It felt like an emergency to me.

Favourite

You're my *favourite*

and that comes with a full stop.

Not my *favourite* place or scene, that would make you my *favourite* but limited to just one thing

If you were only my *favourite* meal it would just be one flavour,

and even the ingredients are small compared to the way in which I favour

You.

On your good days and even more on your bad, you're my *favourite*, especially on those days when you feel sad,

not just when you're great and you're living on a high

But when you're on the floor, those are the times you deserve me much more

You're my *favourite* creation, maybe that's how I can explain it?

As that embodies your entirety and that in which you've been created

From every cell in your body to every strand of your

hair, you're my *favourite* and that's not limited to a type or just one layer

You're my *favourite*. And that comes with a full stop.

Written in dedication to

my little sister Bahar

Forever

Maybe I misunderstood when you said you'd love me
forever

By forever you meant until the leaves fall off the trees
or until the sun came out
and made things look
prettier.

Your forever concluded at a point in time and that was
definitely years and years away from mine.

But truly I wonder if your forever ever really began,
because I don't have a memory without a lie and I
can't seem to remember the last time you didn't make
me cry.

It's not a vision of happiness that stayed in my mind in
fact it hurts to think of it so now I turn a blind eye

So . . . maybe I misunderstood when you said you'd
love me forever.

Mothers

When they ask me who's the luckiest
I tell them it's the *Mothers*
For the *Mother* has a capacity to love far
Greater than the others
If she has a son it will be the last man
She ever falls for with her soul
And if she has a daughter she'll give her everything
She ever needed for her own console
They go through so much trying to raise us and they
Push us forward when we cry
And they cry more but in secret while they praise us
Once their faces dry
The love they have for us is unbreakable
Even though sometimes we break them
We claim they overstepped the walls of our boundaries
even though we overstretched the walls of
Her womb to give US life and so . . . she pretends . . .
To not be hurt, to be respectful of what we
THINK we need and gives us the room to grow

But the *Mother* is the luckiest and she says . . .

"

One day they
will know

"

I'm the Problem

No one knows my darkness and you know what it's not
a problem
If when they tell you about me they say I'm the problem,
then I'm the problem
I no longer run to defend myself I let people think what
they want to think
And if that means they validate me with lies you and I
both know YOU are the weakest link
So when I lay my head down at night I won't be restless
and nor will I cry
But you, YES YOU
Your mind won't be still for long enough for you to
contemplate closing your eyes
You see sleep requires peace and peace is too Holy for
the one that bears untruths on the tongue
For it's attached to the mind, your lies' chain reaction is
the trigger that's been pulled on that gun
Good hearts always win, in this life or the next a cold
heart does not give life
So when you speak of me next time, remember, it's in
YOUR best interest to TRY and be KIND.

People always tell me

to ask God for forgiveness

. . . But what if I don't forgive Him

Lesson

I wish I could understand the lesson God put me here for so I could activate my blessing and free myself from my depression

I wish I could understand the purpose of life, wait, the purpose of MY life, so I could bring meaning to the reason I should "keep on believing"

And no one explained to me the purpose of peace, it wasn't in the books I was given or part of revision, but when I felt it, man, peace is relief

Why didn't anyone show me that sad is just a feeling and most of the time for no reason,

Just a chemical imbalance or the unbalancing of a life that you think you chose, yet you cry every night . . .

I want to know why I am ill-prepared, am I sick? Or just scared, into thinking my dreams are too big. I'm supposed to work, get married and produce kids so who cares?

Who cares about my purpose or what I'm destined to do
who cares about my mind when I don't have a clue
Who I am, what I'm here for and what was the point?
when I've experienced more loss than love at this point

I WANT TO KNOW

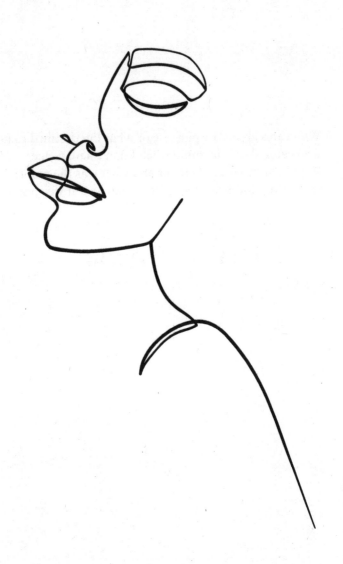

Once you lose access to me don't expect the same version
of me in return

expect the version of me YOU deserve.

From the energy   YOU created.

~ *lose access*

777

I wish there was an emergency line between here and Heaven, so I could make a call and just speak to you for a second, it's not always open just a portal for when you need it and to get through I'd dial *777*

I wish there was a way I could tell you about my day and all the little irrelevant things you cared about that no one else did. Because now when they happen I go to pick up the phone and say but there's no one that would care like you did

I wish I could just say "Hey". That's it. Nothing else. And hear you say your "Hey" back. I imagine my heart would stop skipping that beat and I'd finally be able to breathe and relax

I don't think it's too much to ask for, do you? I can reach anyone I want in the world. But when it comes to you no matter what I do, I beg mercy and still not a word

I pick up the phone and I dial away and I get an answerphone I've heard 206 times. Like the bones in my body dialled one time each thinking one part of me would get a reply

So I'll keep on wishing and I'll keep on trying. I'll probably try for the rest of my life. And I'll make it someday and I'll forever be known as

The One That Could Talk To The Sky

The Last Goodbye

It Doesn't Always Come With Age

Sometimes The First Is As Close As The Last

But It Matters Not When This Day Comes To The
Heaviness For The Heart

The Hands Could Not Create More Fate And The Feet
Had Far To Go

The Predetermination Of Our Time Is Something We
Will Never Know

When We Get To Heaven I'm Sure We'll Ask

The Meaning And The Whys

And The People We Leave Our Pieces With

Will Cry Feeling Left Behind

Some Will Forget Us Within A Week And Some

Take Months And Years

Some Will Never Overcome Our Absence And If We're
Lucky

Our Name Is Within Their Tears

We Spend Our Hours And Our Days

We Spend Our Money And Our Lives

But The Only Spend That Truly Matters Is

How We Spend Our Time

The Last Hour To The Last Minute

The Last Second To The Last Sigh

Our Value Is In The Depth That's Felt

When We Say Our Last Goodbye

Written in dedication to

Tristan Laine Corbett

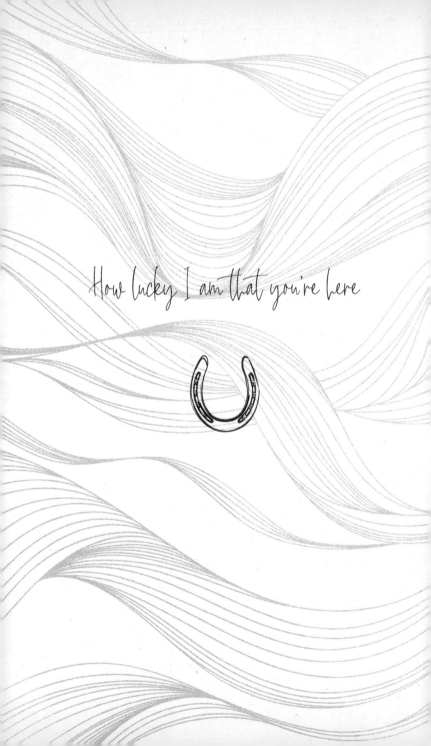

How lucky I am that you're here

Cheating Hearts

I didn't leave you because I wanted to
I still loved you with every ounce of my being
I left you because my heart needed saving
I was so lost in being loyal to you that I didn't realise
How long I had betrayed me for, and the saddest part
is when I left you, my heart did not come with me.
It took years for my heart to stop betraying me
because it was me who had taught it how to cheat.

Will You Remember Me When I Die

Will I be like the ink on a piece of paper that can never be unwritten or will I be a forget me not, where the "not" was forgotten to be written?

Will you remember the sound of my voice or will the memory become non-existent?

Remember the feeling of my tone and the depth, or will my soundwave ~ become straight – like it never existed?

What about my smell? We know that one's easy to tell

Will you remember or will you need a reminder?

So in the essence of that word, need to bring a smell to your nose so that your mind can be reminded?

Have I lived a life worth remembering, to be hard wired in your brain, or am I soft and shapeless?

Am I engraved in the depth of your memory, or is it just my name on a bracelet?

Will you remember me when I die?

I hope so. But don't cry. I don't want your eyelashes to become as heavy as dumbbells with the weight of me

Think of me then let me go. Remember me but don't fall deep into sorrow

If you cry, cry tears of joy, and let the weight of me be your motivation for so much more, because even when I'm gone I know . . . I will remember you.

People think that just because you
saved yourself once upon a time
that the battle is over. They don't
understand that you have to save
yourself every single day. The beast is
always lurking.

They're so naive.

And I don't always win.

Happy New Year

Happy New Year to anyone that had to leave someone behind this year

It may seem like you're leaving a part of you behind but it's just the end of the chapter, not the end of the book

When we meet people we think this person is really on the same page as me, and so we start to write a story, together

But sometimes the story remains unfinished and the book is left with empty pages. It's as if by magic you're supposed to go to bed on New Year's Eve and be renewed on New Year's Day, unbroken and full of resolution.

You don't need to enter the new year without the book, just without that story. The story will continue but for now the book needs to rest on the shelf.

You just need to remember that *You Are The Book*.

And although the story continues without them, it will never continue without you.

Sheeple

Your personality is confusing to people

They don't get that you're a some One
not One of sheeple

It's distressing for them to see you walk your own path

So they get their knives out and try to cut your journey
in half

When really deep down it's just jealousy
They think

"How dare you be an individual when I'm not capable of
breaking free!

How dare you follow your own path while I tread in
others' footsteps and radiate in your light when I can't
see past this darkness!"

But if you let them in they'll only abuse it, for lack of
knowledge on how to use it

So you keep your explanations to yourself and deal with
the hatred that perpetuates

Because you know they can't help the lack in them
and the negative energy that creates

But if they ever want to learn, tell them I'll be here to
teach you

Because the divine in you, it can't be touched by people.

The Way I Used To

I don't cry the way I used to,

but that doesn't mean I'm not as sad,

it just means that the pain is deeper.

Actually, I'm more hurt now because I'm more aware

My mind used to cry whilst my heart kept me safe

But now . . .

my mind keeps me safe, while my heart cries.

One Last Time

Can I Hear Your Voice Call Out My Name

The Sound Of You Travelling Through My Empty Veins

Just Make My Heart Feel Like One Piece Again

Who Do I Write To In Heaven To Get This Consent?

Can I Just Hear For One Second The Sound Of Your Laughter

I'll Put Down This Weapon Of Woe Straight After And

Not Ask For Anything Else Thereafter

I'll Move Peacefully And Un-War Myself From This Disaster

I Will Not Cry At Night And Not Scream Your Name

I Will Not Wish For Endings To Unbreak This Pain

I Will Promise To Stitch Up Every Scar And Unpaint

Your Face From My Nightmares I Will Become Unstained

Can I Just Have *One Last Time?*

Get Well Soon

The three words that are used more often than I love you

But the problem is we're not well and it's already "soon"

The prescriptions of our lives seem to go on for so long that I wonder . . . who is prescribing to who?

And I do, get well soon, for a period of time,

Unless we're referring to the wellness I don't have in my mind. That's a different story

And as much as I am told to get well soon I'm never told when I truly need it and why?

Because nobody can see it

And we wish, to hear those words, so we're seen without the drama and collapse of our bodies because this means, they noticed !?

We have medication to replace the miseducation that in fact we are able and capable of curing ourselves

The people that poison our minds to believe that without these pills we'll never be free

Are the same ones who hope that WE "*get well soon*"

How soon is soon?

It's said with such ease, it's not a prayer or the time taken to contribute to the wellness of me

Just a sentence because they are also at *dis - ease*

They're struggling the same as You and Me and so collectively all that We can hope

is that WE . . . *get well soon.*

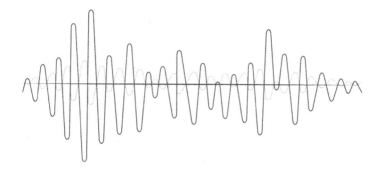

This next poem I wrote whilst I was in a mental institute in 2010 ~ It was published in their weekly magazine.

I was a patient for 2 years – I was told it was only going to be a 4 week stay . . .

This is the first time it will be read since then.

On Top But Holding It Down

We hurt, we heal, we climb and steal
from poor for rich to give even keel

We try and remain, try harder to refrain
from doing the things that are inhumane

We fight from weakness and run to strength
to try and stop ourselves from descent, into the darkness
of what life could be
if we let go we'll never be free

We try and do what's right by the young, innocent and
pure they have only begun, to open their
ears and listen with eyes and decipher the
truth from all of the lies

We lead by example and hold our heads high
we hurt when we're pinched but try not to cry
for fear of judgement or too much pride
that shadows the emotion that we shouldn't hide

We're born, we live, some to extreme
we ride the waves and live the dream
we find likes and dislikes and build our own fort
we find ways to attract and ways to retort

We are only human, human within
human outside and human with sin

Human with faith and human with flaw
But nonetheless human and nothing more

So live your life how you want to be
live your life to every degree
take too much and laugh too loud
fight for your rights and be overly proud

At every success and every goal
every achievement and every result
open your eyes and feel alive

I want to live,

not merely survive.

There are people in this world that don't have an inner
narrative . . . this blew my mind when I found this out.
The

first thing I felt was envy. How freeing must that be?
To

not have to convince your voice in your head to be
Your

friend. To not think a thousand thoughts a minute and
Listen

to agonising comments about yourself day after
Day.

But then I thought . . .

How lonely.

Left Behind

I don't blame you for leaving us

Every day I want to leave too

The way you left was the hardest for me

But probably the easiest for you

I think back to that night, night after night

The what ifs the whys and what I didn't say

The people around me will never understand the noise of this silent pain

My eyes are different now, and so is my voice. The way I see things has changed

If only I knew then what I know now and had the chance to ask you to stay

Come on Dad. I screamed it, I even smiled. Not for a second could I comprehend

That in that moment everything as I knew it, the world and my heart, with your heart, had come to an end.

~ *a true story*

Give and Take

Givers have to set limits because
Takers rarely do

Being a selfless person is a tough
thing when it comes to knowing the
meaning of
too much before you've already
hit empty.

You shut down your own feelings,
needs and events on
any given day to rescue another
without a second thought,
as this is a natural pattern for you.

Doing this is ok until you realise
when you asked there was silence.

When you pushed through
there was no reflection and when you
were in darkness there was no light.

Don't be afraid to ask for what you need,
but don't be a fool to ask twice.

Don't repeat yourself and don't let this pattern become a
habit.

It's tough, I know.
It's hard to be assertive when we're
naturally wired to give, love and please.

But someone has to cut the cord and as the
"Giver"
it's going to have to be you.
As Takers rarely do.

Born Still

I remember the day I saw your face, it was the first and it was the last

All I wanted was to hear your voice, or the sound of a beating heart

I prepared my life and my soul for your presence, but very little did I know

That this world was not ready to have you in it, I said goodbye at the same time as hello

My heart, my world, my mind all shattered, the pieces I will never regain

I would give my life for your life, my heart for your heart, anything to see your face again

Your clothes unworn, your room unused, the moments I never got to see

I met you for a second, an eternal love will remain, but you never got to meet me.

Enough

Don't ever forget that you are *enough*

Especially when the world is feeling too *rough*

When the cards you've been dealt are feeling so *tough*

And the choices you didn't make are hurting too *much*

Don't ever forget your place in this *world*

No matter how many mistakes you still *deserve*

To be here like the rest of us and continue to *learn*

That nobody's perfect and we're all a little *hurt*

We all have scars and secrets we don't *share*

We all have burdens too heavy to *bear*

When we disappear sometimes it seems like we don't *care*

But really we're just trying to find our way *home*.

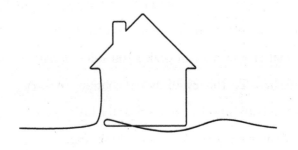

Good Time Friend

I am not the "good time friend".

I am not the person that people call when they want to go out and have a great time.

I'm the person people call when they're tired of fighting their demons on their own . . . and because of that . . .

My phone does not ring very often.

*~ Some people love playing with
their demons too much*

Black and Blue

When I say black and blue

What do you think of?

Is it the sky? The dark or the moon?

Does it make you think of the ocean at night?

Do you separate the colours in two?

It doesn't give you a good feeling does it . . .

In fact it doesn't make you think of any place at all

It doesn't incite a memory of laughter

It makes the smile from your face fall

There's the black and blue that got away with it

And the black and blue no one knows

There's the black and blue that stained your spirit

And the black without the blue on your soul

They say that to love is to touch one's heart

In time

To love is to never cause pain

But love sometimes can blind us

Of the one truth

Love is a drug and you are the addict again

~ DV

True freedom is when you can sit in a room by yourself,

and think nice things.

Seen

I want a love that will make me fall apart
But not in the literal sense, I mean in the barrier sense
I want to tear every boundary down and expose
everything about what I've done wrong
No remorse. No fear. Just flaws.

I want a love that makes me break me in order to be a
better person for you
Because the simple thought of losing you to keeping me
is unbearable
Inhale. Exhale. Change.

I want to lose interest in everything I once thought to be
interesting and realise that for so long I was no longer
investing until it came to you
The expense of you will feel like freedom because to love
you is so cheap it's free
And my friends will get sick of hearing about it, some of
them may not come back around but they don't get it
I prayed. I waited. I isolated.

For you.
And now. Now you are here and here I am.
Breaking my barriers, dropping my guards because the
way you look at me makes me feel like I've never been
seen before.

A Day of Valentine

Happy Valentine's Day to my Mum
and to all the Mum's and Dad's that don't get to spend
this day with the love of their life anymore

My Dad never used to buy anything for my Mum when
we were growing up, he would always say "why do I need
to buy that stuff, I'm here every day . . ." and he was,
but we knew she cared

When we got older we started to buy things for her and
write his name in it, we played with his conscience for
years until he knew that this was something he should be
doing. He started to buy things himself and every time
he gave her something he would always laugh . . . and so
would we

My Dad was a real man's man and he never really got
used to being affectionate. Just as he flourished to his
peak, he was gone . . .

Happy Valentine's Day and don't you feel the loss of love
today. For you have experienced a greater love than most
people in our generation ever really will. And although
the body may be gone, that love . . . that true love.

It lives on within you forever

"

I waited for so long for
people to notice that
I was drowning

And they didn't.

"

And one day with no warning, there will come a day

where you will never hear my voice again.

And when that day comes I want you to know something

You were enough.

You did enough.

You said enough.

And I knew every day that you loved me.

~ A letter to my little sister

Permission

I give myself permission to let you go
Never forgetting but no longer forsaking my own
happiness

With the guilt that I feel for
moving on without you
I give myself permission to smile
And to not punish myself for
doing so

You will forever live in my heart
But my mind deserves to rest.

Wasn't Enough

I loved you and it wasn't enough

I wasn't enough

At least that's what I told myself day after day for years

I didn't realise that the way that you treated me was not a reflection on me

You would have done what you did

No matter who I was

No matter how I treated you

And I blamed myself and I blamed myself

Until there was nothing left of me and yet I still saw everything in you

That's how much I loved you.

Overnight

I didn't fall in love with you overnight

It wasn't fast like a car on a motorway

It happened slowly, like when you try and run underwater

And just like a ship can't sink unless you have more
water in it than around it

My heart sank in the ocean that is you.

The hardest break-up a heart has
to endure is

an unwanted break-up from a best
friend.

Not Anymore

We're not friends anymore and I know it but I haven't said anything to you.

I haven't even unfollowed your social media even though if a picture of yours comes up I just scroll, I don't look.

And the thing is I don't unfollow you because I don't want to let **you** down. But when you let me down it didn't even matter to you.

I don't want to break your heart because when you broke my heart it was just one heart that was broken but if I break yours, it will be mine too.

Memory Loss

They call it memory loss but I don't think you can
ever lose a memory.
Somewhere inside you it still exists you just don't
know where it is anymore.
It becomes part of the lost and found area because it's
not where you left it.
So even if you search for it you can't find it because
a part of you found it
and removed it to keep you safe.
Each time you go to collect it you're told it's not
there, but you remember where you left it,
just not where you put it.

Light Up

There are people in this world whose faces light up when they see you.

And that's not because of what you can do or what you can provide or how they can benefit from you.

It's just because of who you are.

She doesn't need you. She never needed you.

She wanted you. She gave you the opportunity to become a piece of her, not to destroy the peace in her. Anything that She needs She can provide for herself. So all you had to do was be exactly who you said you would be.

And if you cannot lead her to peace . . . Then She will leave you in pieces.

He doesn't need you. He never needed you.

He wanted you. He gave you the opportunity to become a piece of him, not to destroy the peace in him.

Anything that He needs He can provide for himself. So all you had to do was be exactly who you said you would be.

And if you cannot lead him to peace . . . Then He will leave you in pieces.

AND DON'T YOU EVER FORGET

How they gave you distance

When you needed LOVE

One of the hardest things about healing is that the version of yourself that you became in order to get through the war that you were presented with is also somebody that you have to let go of. See, the version of yourself that you had to be in order to survive is not the version of yourself that you can now be to continue. You have to leave that version of yourself behind. So it's a double edged sword, you have to create someone to get through it but once you're over that hill you can't take that person with you. That person was for the war and the war is now won.

The battle may continue. But they can not.

WAR

Gone

I now know that you're gone, and there is nothing I can do to bring you back

and I don't know if it's more or less painful than when I thought this wasn't real and that maybe there was something I could do.

I now know that we are destined to lose the people we love . . .

and I can only hope that there are people in this world that would be as sad to lose me, as I was to lose you.

People don't remember what you say to them. They
remember how you make them feel.
The beauty in
your face gives a first impression . . . But the beauty in
your character leaves a lasting impression.

It's not always easy to be kind to people all the time,
some people really don't deserve it. And no it may not
put money in your bank. But the way people
remember you . . .

That's your legacy

∞ REMEMBER ME ∞

Pause

Give me a minute.

Yes I know I'm the strongest person you know and if anyone can do it I can, but your glorifying of my trauma does not mean that I don't feel it

Can you give me a second?

Because it's been one after another lately I just don't talk to you about it anymore, but I don't need your force to be the force I need to reckon

Give me some time

To gather up my thoughts you don't know what it takes to be me and I make it look so easy, yeah I'm sure

Give me some room

From the version of me you desperately want and I beg you stop telling me what I need to do when you literally have no clue

I don't need to be the version you see as the best

Sometimes that person disappears if I don't take the time to rest

And if I felt I needed anything from you I'd say it but I don't

I just need a minute. So please.

Leave me alone.

But darling . . .

Love doesn't hurt the way they

hurt you.

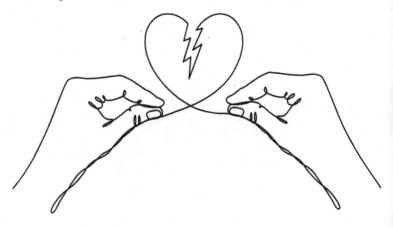

They say that grief is just love with no place to go. It feels like you can implode at any second. What am I supposed to do like this? How am I supposed to function?

If grief is just love . . . then why does it hurt so bad?

~ *midnight thoughts*

Imagine

Imagine a world where colour didn't exist
What would happen then I wonder . . .
Would the segregation still continue
or would we live in union?
No ethnic box to come under
Imagine if we all lived in harmony and
our skin was seen as a superpower
but not the colour just the layers
And everyone has it so we're all magicians
We're all just by one creator

Imagine if we couldn't see a difference
How peaceful would that be?
Imagine if there was no religion
Just God, and we understood unity
In a colourless world we would just see features and
everyone has a nose
Different shapes and sizes heights and eyes
fingers and toes

Imagine that

Sounds so surreal that we could live in such a way
And when you realise it's not because of society
but your own choices . . . those things you say
You'll be forgiven just so you know
because some people are already living in this way
and they'll show you
. . . if you want
They will
show you
the
way

My Favourite Quote

___

" Some people can't
support you in public
because of the way
they speak about
you in private. "

A Someone

You are somebody's someone.

In a room full of a thousand people
they would pick you.

And they wouldn't just pick you when you feel perfect.

They would pick you with every single one of your
imperfections too.

The devil will show up as a person you love
everything about . . . and destroy you.
God will show up as a person that will hurt you with
the truth, so that you can move on from anything
that's not for you.

~ *DISCERNMENT*

You leave them where you found them.

Keep Walking

And one day when you realise what you've done, what you let go of and what you lost.

Don't. You. Dare.

Turn back around.

Buried Alive

Some people die in your life while they're still alive,
and in some ways it's harder to grieve for them,
because the choice to see them is still here.

So you have to wake up every day and choose not to
go where your heart desires the most.

Leaving someone you love is one of the hardest things
you'll ever have to do.

You can only be in pain where you were once in love.

. . . Pain equals love plus truth.

Rise Down

I don't know why everyone's talking about the great
uprising,
we don't deserve God

Everyone's running around serving a religion that
serves a God, that doesn't serve God

You wanna know why God doesn't stop all evil but
what about the evil that's in you?

Because if God was to stitch up every mouth that told
a lie . . . he would stitch yours too.

Here we go again..

You knew this was coming..

But I don't understand..

You don't need to..

~ Mind vs Heart

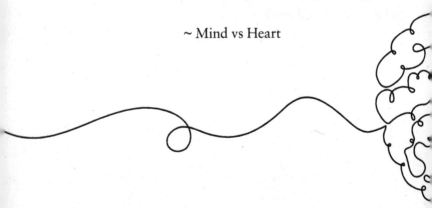

True North

Keep people in your life that have the consistency
of the North Star

You can't always see it . . . but every night . . .

You know it's there.

Debt

I think I will have certain regrets for the rest of my
life.

It took me taking your life for granted to
understand to not *take* mine.

If time was a currency, and God counted how much I
had wasted, I wonder . . .

I wonder if He will ask for it back . . .

The Skin I'm In

I have never learnt how to be comfortable in
my own skin

I spent my whole childhood obsessed with being thin

I would draw my bones on pieces of paper and stare in
the mirror for hours

But my eyes I would not dare to look in

Even when I do my makeup I don't actually look at me

I just look at a load of imperfections and feel
embarrassed by what people must see

They tell me if only you could see you through my eyes

But the thought of this terrifies me so much because
what if I'm *STILL* this ugly

I know beauty is within so I worked on my soul

and my soul is as good as gold, this part I know

But not all humans are capable of seeing this as equal,
they measure in inches and tell me "you've grown"

I don't know if I'll ever be good enough for this world

but what if this world isn't good enough for me?

What if I'm the one that's ok and the problems I see are created from the eyes of the critiques

So if I remove their voices from my brain and their opinions from my mind's eye

it's a problem I'll no longer see

Maybe just maybe in the next world I'll be pretty

But not pretty to you

I'll be pretty to me.

Served

I wanted different, so I stopped treating myself like
I was a takeaway. People would come into my life, fill up
their boxes,
take their bags and leave.

So I became a restaurant . . .

And if you don't have a table, you can't eat here.

Space

Somewhere in between Love and Hate, there's Us.

Now, I don't know what to call that . . .

Is it medium? And if it is medium, who wants medium?

Surely it can't be nothing, because it's impossible to feel nothing

Even the art of feeling nothing means that you're feeling something

So it's just a space.

You take up a space in me.

And I don't know what to call it.

Stay Soft

Don't ever let them win

They may have broken your heart, but they don't get

to break your soul.

Commitment Issues

And that's the problem with this life . . .

People just want to look at *things*
Without *committing*
To one *thing*
Because they're just *acting*
And they're not *understanding*
They're just *reacting*
To a bunch of *feelings*
Without deeper *meaning*
So once that's *dispersing*
They're just *moving*
Onto the next *thing*
Without love *developing*
Because love takes *reasoning*
Without the *seasoning*
Of everyday life *things*
You're meant to be *building*
Together and *listening*
To what they are *needing*
But we're all *leaving*
The moment that funny *feeling*

Is leaving too.

"

Some people think that
because you show up
in peace . . .

You're not ready for War.

"

The Best is Yet to Come

And I hope you choose to heal

And when you choose to heal I hope you understand that you will lose the people you love

And when you lose the people you love I hope you understand that you will feel broken instead of healing

And when you feel broken I hope you choose to stay the path, I hope you choose to believe in yourself and believe in your journey

And understand that the best . . .

. . . *Is Yet To Come*

I'm Sorry

I'm *sorry* you missed the divine in me

I'm *sorry* you missed out on the person that I am and

I am so *sorry* that you didn't realise how amazing my soul is

I'm *sorry* you wasn't ready, and you missed out on loving me and you settled for far less and watched me become, far more

I forgive you.

And I only hope, one day, you find a way . . .

   To forgive yourself.

Depreciation

He told me he loved me and I told him, I loved him
too

He told me he would never lose me and I said you
never could too

He said he hated the way I overthink and don't get
over things and I said . . . I hated him too

He told me he loved me before he knew me and I
said, I found out who you were and love means

I still loved you.

Old School Love

You see I want that old school love, that RnB love

That pick me up if I'm wearing heels, kinda love

That send me a song and say at one minute twelve this line reminds me of you, kinda love

That don't worry we'll get through this together kinda love

That where shall we go, no let's just drive as long as we're together, old school love

I want that lie in the car and look at the stars kinda love

I want that *old school love*

7 Stages of Grief

The 7 stages of grief.

That's what they call it right? But really they should call it the 7 cycles of grief.

A stage has an end but grief has no end, by the time you finish you just start again

And even if you are free of that heart wrenching pain for a few days, the guilt that you will feel, you will throw yourself straight back into cycle 1

Here we go again . . .

But don't ever underestimate how lucky you are if you cry for the rest of your life

Some people never get to experience a love like that

They may not be here anymore, but that love

It will never die.

denial

guilt

anger

depression

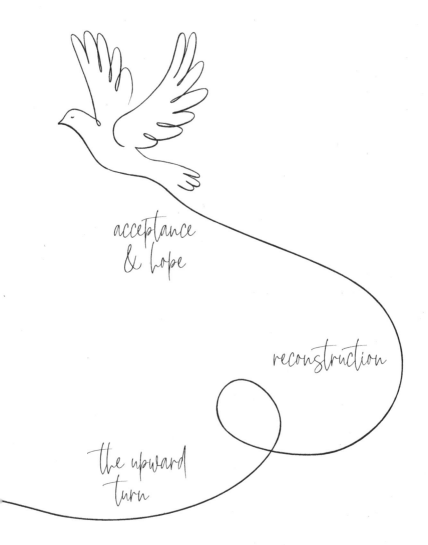

acceptance
& hope

reconstruction

the upward
turn

And I don't regret it, not for a second

You needed that love and you needed that light

And in order to heal you I had to break me

But it's ok . . . that love and that light . . . belongs to me.

~ mine

1+1

We used to be a part of each other

But now we're just apart from each other

You were my + 1

My 2 + 2

My what 4

My 8 in Gr8

There was never 1 without the Other

But now we don't know each other

After all that we're just strangers

We're just the strange in eSTRANGEd

And I wish we could go back

You were You.
I was Me.
We were happy when we were
We.

Comfort. I really like this word. The word itself feels soft. You are supposed to feel safe, like in the comfort of your own home, they gave me comfort, I felt comfort in that, it gave me comfort to know that. But I don't know if I've ever felt it.

Swim for Me

You can't rescue somebody that doesn't want to be saved

Don't feel bad for walking away from someone that doesn't want to be saved

You can stretch your arms out to someone from a boat and say "Get out of the water!"

They pull you in the water and now you're drowning, who saves you?

Remember these words . . .

      I said I'd swim for you.

          I never said I'd drown for you.

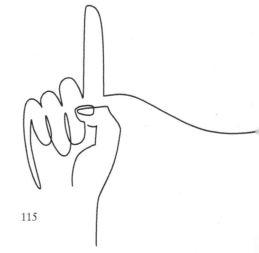

I wish somebody had told you

I wish somebody had told you, how proud they are of you and how beautiful you are when it would have been easy for you to accept it, rather than now, when it is a fight to get you to even believe it

I wish somebody had told you when you were young enough to accept everything that everyone said so that it would have been channelled into your mindset

And in case you needed to hear that today you are beautiful and you are loved and your place in this world

. . .

It can only be taken by you.

~ a letter to little me

Relentless

I know that God sees my heart. But I also know that
He sees that I'm tired.

I am so tired.

And because I'm tired my mind is unfaithful.

I can't get it to trust in anything.

I just hope that my heart is strong enough to win.

Anxiety

I suffered so badly with anxiety
With the voices that went off inside of me
And I would tremble in my hands and
I couldn't breathe hear or see
It would literally block all my sinuses

I had to know all things at all times
My future needed to be predicted
Trailing through the horoscopes
To tell me about my day
The tarots, the cards
I was addicted

Every second was a thought and
Every thought had a second I felt like
I was going insane

And I'd look at people in total calmness and say
"Yes why"
When they'd ask me if I'm ok

God forbid I'd let anyone in
Can you imagine what they would think of me?

No no no
I can't tell the truth I have an image
I need to maintain

If they look at me the wrong way
I'll physically fall over from the overthinking
This will cost me it's too expensive

To even start this conversation is
Too overwhelming the damage is far too extensive
No.

I'll just stay quiet.

Well only on the outside . . . because inside

It's never quiet.

It's never quiet.

Brave

I think it's BRAVE.

I think it's really brave what you did and what you
continue to do every day.
Some people never have the courage to move, they
never even leave their hometown.

So I think it's brave. I think you're brave.

Submissive

I want to be submissive. So many people these days
act as if being submissive is a bad thing but it can't be.
To feel safe enough to drop my guard?
To feel comfortable enough to be vulnerable and
allow someone else to take over? Wow.

I can't wait to be submissive.

Changing People

Don't try and change people!

Don't you try and change people!

Let them show you their character.
Let them show you their qualities.
Let them show you their behaviour AND
Let them stop you from wasting your

God
       Given
              Time.

Hopeful

I hope that you fall in love and
it hurts so bad

I hope your heart is destroyed and
depleted and you feel beyond sad

Because it means you've experienced
the greatest pain but also the greatest gift

Without love the meaning of life
is just a myth

It won't be the first and it may not be the last
but I promise you your heart will
heal itself and without the broken
we stay in the dark

Because the cracks are needed for the light to get in.

Healing is a gift you give yourself. Most of the time people don't do it for two reasons . . .

1. They don't want to go through the pain
      and
2. They don't feel like they deserve it

~ which one are you

Grown-ups

We're grown-ups now, and that means
we don't have as much free time as we used to.

But I want you to know that I think about you all the
time.
There is a piece
of my heart that belongs to you.

We're all just actors playing in our own
movies and I am so glad
that you played a role in mine.

I will not be getting revenge on anyone that did me dirty.

I will just set an example by winning on another level without doing anyone else dirty.

We are not fighting trauma with trauma.

The Cycle Ends With Me.

Disrespect

One of the highest forms
of manipulation is when people call
you mad when you react to

d
i
s
r
e
s
p
e
c
t

Stay

You do not want to die.

You want something in you to end.
You want the pain to end.
You want the thoughts to end.
You want the feeling to end.

You don't understand how final death really is.

You may think the world would be a better place without
you in it
but I **promise** you
somebody's world will never be the same
if you are not here.

If you have to make a choice

today

I hope you choose to stay.

I HOPE YOU CHOOSE TO STAY

That's not love.

That's pain and confusion and imbalance and neglect,

that's disrespect and dishonesty, that's inconsistency

and broken promises, that's heavy on forgiveness and

heavier on betrayal, that's bullying and THAT's

harassment, that's manipulation.

We don't suffer for love. It may be many things, but . . .

That's not love.

Shock

_____

I think I'm still in shock. It's been years and I am still
in shock and I hate it.
Because I want to feel every inch of my sadness right
the way through my bones

and I can't

. . . and I know I should be grateful for I would
surely die from a pain like that.

So I just feel some of it sometimes, too much of it at
night time, but never all of it.

Never all of losing you, all the time.

If I could have burnt
the entire world down
with my grief . . .

I would have.

I'll Hold Space for You

I think there will be a piece missing from me for the rest
of my life . . .

and although I try and fill it with people or things,
I know I will always feel that void . . .

. . . and maybe that's what they mean when they say

"I'll Hold Space For You"

because that space will always be yours.

The biggest fail is when people don't learn to not carry on the behaviours that broke them.
They continue the cycle using the excuse, well they broke me . . .

~ Disappointment

Good Hearts

I have never understood why Good Hearts finish last,
why people hurt people and why
God gives his hardest battles to his toughest soldiers.

I hope if I ever come back one day, I come back to a
different world, where all the great people
live the easiest lives and have the best of
everything they deserve.

Someone once told me that our tears are little
prayers that God listens to and that stayed with me . . .
and if that's the truth, God has listened to me more
than a billion times.

~ *a billion prayers*

She's a 10 but . . .

She randomly goes back to depressive episodes every
time things start to get better, because she finds so
much comfort in her own mental illness.

~ still a 10

Too Easy

You wanted to say something bad about me
so you attacked the way I look and

bitch that's too easy

You wanted to defame my character but
you know I'm good as gold and even if you
ignore my personality you

can't ignore my soul

You're desperately trying to expose me and
you're getting mad because you keep
coming up empty

I'm not who you see me as that's
your reflection and my kindness is living in

your head rent free

You're reading your bible and going to
church but in life you're acting

Ungodly

And it eats away at you day and night that
a person can still treat you

Godly

And just like the sun the moon and the stars
the truth never stays hidden

You're gonna learn the hard way one day that evil on the
tongue is

strictly forbidden

Real Eyes
     Realise
          Real Lies

I first wrote this quote twelve years ago. It took death and twelve years for me to really understand the meaning of it. You will never feel more pain in the pit of your stomach than when you find out someone you love has betrayed you. Family being the worst ones. I always used to listen to the stories of arguments over money when people died but I never thought that could be my family. We were so close. I grew up in a really big group of cousins and I don't speak to any of them anymore. When my Dad died some of them came after my Mum like vultures. For land that we didn't even care about, for money we didn't even have and whilst my Dad's body was still warm. I will never be more ashamed of anyone than I am of some members of my own family. They ripped what was left of my soul out of me.

Belong

I don't belong here.
I never have done and I never will do, and that's ok.
I've come to terms with that.
I've had this insatiable feeling of wanting to go home
since I was a kid.
I know that "Home" is not a place that's in this world.
You're not the only one.

Pretty privilege does not exist without negative consequences. There was not a single environment that I grew up in that was "safe". There was not a single person that I came across that was not trying to do something that was against my will. Please do not fall for the things people are flaunting online, I can guarantee you that there are tears that are being shed behind closed doors of the things that they're having to endure that they don't want to.

Be careful what you wish for . . .

All that glitters is not gold

No Good

I shoot myself in the foot by doing things for people
that would never do the same for me,
and no matter how many times
I've seen that I need to leave this person behind,
I think but they're a good person.
I use that excuse to allow the behaviour to
continue without seeing that although
yes they may be a good person,
they're not a good person to me.

Overcome

One thing about me is I'm gonna overcome it. I don't
care what it is
I don't care how bad it gets, I don't care what you did
to me and what you thought.

I'm gonna overcome it.
And they will sit there in shock and say surely she
can't continue after that one, but I will.

I will.

God's Favourite

I want to be God's favourite . . .

And yeah that may be a little selfish

And I probably don't deserve it because

He knows how many mistakes I've made

But I didn't quit.

Never once did I quit.

I hope when He looks at me He says

"You see that One

She resembles what I originally intended."

They broke your spirit, you lost yourself and I lost you. If I could have found the part that was missing . . .

I searched the world to try and find the part that was missing so I could give it back to you and take away your emptiness. But it was lost. Now without you, I don't know if I will ever be found again.

"Un-Alive"

Solitude

She's at a place in her life where you're no longer competing with other people to be with her. You're competing with her Peace.

Her solitude is so comfortable.
So if you want to be in her life, you're going to need to show her the reasons
WHY
that noise that you are making is better than the silence that she has earned.

Half of Me

They wanted me to leave him everybody wanted me to leave him but

        How

            Do

                I

                    Leave

                        Him.

He was the entire source of my happiness, I put all the power into his hands he was everything that I thought that I needed . . . and he made me feel like he was

      Half of Me

When he wasn't even

      Half of Me

Because he fed off of

      Half of Me

To try and even be a

      Half of Me.

It amazes me how someone can make YOU feel sad
but you're not allowed to talk about how sad they
made YOU feel.
Because if you talk about how sad they made YOU
feel, YOU will make THEM feel sad and THAT's
unacceptable.

~ *Double standards*

I don't glorify grief.

There is nothing inspirational about any phase any moment or any milestone. It's not like I'm going to achieve something is it?

"Dear diary today I got over my Dad dying on his bedroom floor??"

There is nothing great in grief. I won't sugar coat it to make myself out to be someone that dealt with something better than others. In fact, I think I have been one of the worst examples. Maybe I feel too much and I love too deeply, I don't know. I see others losing people and getting back to normal in a year and I think HOW!! Could not be me. Year five has been the worst so far, the coherence has made me suffer internally. But year five has definitely taught me that life will not and cannot be the same. And that's ok. It is ok. Why should it be the same? Someone that was a pillar in your life is gone.

Out of respect for the love you had for them, life should never be the same and THAT is ok.

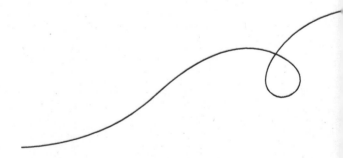

You left before I could make you proud, and every day
I look up at the sky hoping and praying that you're
watching, and the toughest thing is that it doesn't
matter how many people tell me that what I have done
is amazing or how proud they are of me,
I will never get to hear you say it.
So I'll just carry on looking up at the sky, hoping that
one day,

I'll get to hear it again.

~ *Look Up*

I Win

I don't think about you anymore . . . **so I win**

. . . and I know most people associate winning with some sort of celebration. It's cheer and it's loud and there's celebration. But it's not like that, not
for me anyway.

I inhale.

Then I exhale.

And it didn't hurt.

Daughter

They say that the Mother should never
have to be the one to bury her daughter

And a Father will forever blame himself for her pain
as he sees himself as the one that should
have caught her

They say that in this life you will get the chance to
see a "Her" in you

And that chance is sometimes shorter than expected,
even when you did all that you could do

They say that a little girl's laughter could heal
a Mother's broken soul

And her Father will evolve into a man to provide her
the arms that she will call "Home"

If tomorrow starts without her, followed by all the
tomorrows to come

and the emptiness in you is so overwhelming it makes
you feel so numb

I promise you will make it even though you may not
believe

and she will be your driving force with every step as
you proceed

She may not be visible anymore and you may not hear her voice

You may think I can't carry on and be angry at not being given a choice

Fear not the tears that fall inside for she will never be gone

For as long as you stand, with the air in your lungs

A part of her   forever   lives on.

Son

They say that a Mother should never have to
bear the thought of burying her son

And to lower the coffin of his baby boy
into the ground, the Father
should never be the one

They say that the great circle of life means
that the elders always go first

But that's just not the case it seems when a
parent is the one that's alive in the hearse

They say that the son is a Mother's first true love
and to a Father a boy will teach him
how to be a man

To lose a son is to lose your reason to
feel there is anything left to understand

They say that your place in heaven is not guaranteed
but to have a son will make this untrue

For when you give life to a precious boy, an eternal
heaven was created within you

Fear not the tears that fall inside
for he will never be gone

For as long as you stand, with the air in your lungs

A part of him   forever   lives on.

Affirmation

I DESERVE BETTER.

I deserve the love I have given to everyone but me.

I AM the best version of myself that I have ever been, but not yet the best version of myself I will ever be.

I AM learning.

I AM growing.

I WILL become everything I have ever dreamed of.

My favourite thing about the people that
have let me
down is that they gave me a template of
what I would
NEVER want to be.

I watched the pain change them

And I said to myself, "never me"

Nothing and no one will ever have the
power to
change the core of my soul.

Little Me

When you lie in bed at night, and the voices start to appear

And you squeeze your little eyes and you shed a little tear

You hold onto the pillow and curl up in your sheets

And cover up your mouth so no one hears your screams

I won't tell you to ignore them, because they're a part of you you know,

They also need to be heard and be loved, they're also part of your growth

Just give them space to tell you all the things they think and feel

And remind yourself this is the little me that I didn't get to heal.

When people ask me what is my relationship with God
. . .

I reply,

"I have given Him a million reasons to stop loving me,

yet . . .

     He's never left my side."

~ *Unconditional*

*If I mentally fall apart before this book comes out
because of my procrastination, ADHD, mental fog,
general grief, multitude of personalities and inability
to fully execute my ideas due to mental paralysis and
because I think everyone will hate them, please know . . .*

*No one will believe in you until believing in you becomes
popular. No one knows I am writing this book or how
hard it has been for me to actually sit and get through it.
My self doubt has stolen years from me. But discipline
has made me continue in my own face of adversity. I had
a vision that doesn't exist in this world yet . . . as many
of us do, and to follow something like that you have to
be just a little bit crazy.*

Keep quiet and keep moving.

Save My Seat

I work so hard every day of my life for the following reason . . .

I intend on seeing my Dad again and I know a place in heaven is not guaranteed. I know he went to heaven.

He had too good a heart to be taken that young, the devil would have left him here.

So I have to work every day to secure my place in heaven, to get my chance to see him again.

Without You

I don't want to carry on without you.
I work so hard to get to a certain point and just before
I cross the finish line, I stop.
I lose all energy to want to carry on because I know, I
know that crossing that line means creating something
you will never be part of.

I know you would tell me to keep going, but it will
never be ok to do this without you.

"

You didn't come
this far
just to come
this far.

"

Doubt Me

Doubt me yeah I love that *shit*

Tell people I can't make it and watch me create that *shit*

Cause me pain and see what I make from that *shit*

Ridicule me to your friends, but they'll tell you she ate that *shit*

Be the artist of my motivation and watch me paint that *shit*

You think I can't carry on with these scars but I'll just tape that *shit*

Talk to your God about me, cause my God don't play about that *shit*

Keep giving me reasons to grow, cause I can take that *shit*

SO DOUBT ME

Doubt me yeah I love that *shit*

Kind

I was KIND

Even when you didn't deserve it I was
KIND

Even when I heard everything you had said about me

I was KIND

And I wasn't kind because of who YOU are

I was kind because of who I AM

I don't pray for you to be punished

That's too easy

I only pray that I have the courage to continue to be
KIND

No matter what you do.

I hope you win.

I hope you win that war that's going on inside your head that nobody else knows about. I hope you're grateful, to yourself! For everything that you've done for yourself, for not giving up on yourself when everybody else did. I hope you say THANK YOU in the mirror, I hope you say I LOVE YOU in the mirror. Thank you for not quitting on me. I hope you know that everything that you do today is for all of your tomorrows. Everything that you do this year is for your next five years. I hope you drown out the opinions of everybody else around you, because they couldn't, that's why they tell you you can't. They didn't, that's why they tell you don't! Nobody else's opinion matters but yours, you tell yourself every single day thank you.

Thank you for carrying me, thank you for not quitting on me. I hope you win the war. I hope you get there.

   I HAVE FAITH

Everything Sits Still
in the Graveyard

There's the man that comes to visit his wife every day
He sits in his car by her grave and watches the sunrise till
the sun sets
He never leaves. He never leaves.
And the widows that come to visit their husbands and
lay fresh flowers every single week
And then there's the small graves
The ones with all the toys, so colourful, so pretty
But the toys are never played with
They will never be used
People come and go
And some never get to leave

But everything sits still in the Graveyard.

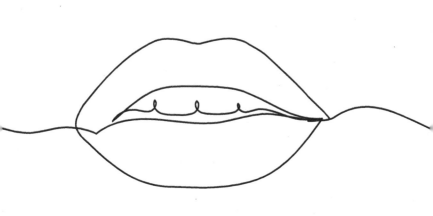

Epilogue

I originally called this book August because it was the month I was born, the month I died and the month I was reborn. I was born on August the 28th. In 2018 we all had dinner for the last time together in my kitchen, for my birthday, on August 27th.

My older sister had left before dinner and randomly decided to drive back. My Mum got home early from work, another random thing. We ordered Domino's pizza. We laughed, a lot. My Dad was divulging all the things he eats in secret and was belly laughing so hard because he thought it was hilarious. He had diabetes so it really wasn't, but I couldn't help but laugh whilst telling him off.

I remember this moment like it was yesterday, he was standing in the living room and I remember thinking *he is so swollen*. He had one of those big protruding Dad bellies with small arms and legs. My Mum leaned over to me and said, "I don't know why he's laughing; I keep getting scared he's going to have a heart attack in his sleep."

I said, "MUM do not say that!! Don't put that into the universe."

I knew what she meant because on August 10th I had a dream Dad had a heart attack. I texted him the next day just checking in, not telling him why. This would be the last lengthy text conversation we ever had. I read it sometimes when I can take it.

So . . . the next day was my birthday, I stopped by the house in the morning and I was on my phone a lot responding to silly Facebook messages. My Dad called me over a few times . . . I said, "Dad! Wait!" He just wanted my attention to show me a few pics he was looking at. This moment of not giving him attention haunts me to this day.

On August 29th I stopped by the house and asked my Dad for his ibuprofen, he had extra strong ones. He was not himself and I knew it. He was anxious. As I walked away, I turned and waved and said goodbye to him. I didn't kiss him goodbye and for that I will never forgive myself. On the night of August 30th, he had a heart attack in his sleep. I begged him to wake up. I kept saying "Come on, Dad". He was pronounced dead on his bedroom floor in front of us at 1.37 a.m.

~ The Last Supper

August 31st 2018

Acknowledgements

The Most High and Almighty.

Plus anyone that's ever caused me pain.

Thank you.

About the Author

This book was written by Havva Ramadan – born and raised in Kent and South London. After enduring one of the toughest upbringings with violence and abuse, she escaped her home at sixteen. Although she always had the voice and the creative talent her environment stopped her from ever having the right surroundings to focus and flourish. Falling into gang culture and all that comes with it – she lost her voice. Her outer voice became an uncontrollable inner voice of pain that she could no longer express out loud. She became silent as her mind took over. For most of her life survival was her priority, until she lost her Dad. Suddenly time became relevant, forgiveness and courage became part of survival and what she once thought was sadness was replaced by the dreaded regret and grief she now carried around in her empty soul. She took to social media to live in real time her grief journey after never finding anything comforting in the excruciating years after his death. In baring her heart every day and showing that grief is not linear, and healing is so traumatising, she hopes to create a safe space for all the other hearts that feel as lonely as hers does.

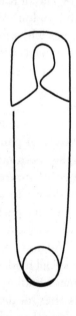